LEADERSHIP, DISTILLED

Twelve Brief Lessons. One Big Impact.

Copyright © 2021 by Catherine Glynn, IngramSpark

Leadership, Distilled
Twelve Brief Lessons. One Big Impact.

Written by Catherine Glynn, MFA
Cover art *Red Focus 1* by Chaco Terada © 2014

Author headshot photography credit Chris Popio

Minnesota, USA
All rights reserved.

No part of this book may be reproduced, transmitted, or stored in an information retrieval system in any form or by any means, graphic, electronic, or mechanical, including photocopying, taping, and recording, without prior written permission from the publisher.
For information email info@voceveritas.com
www.voceveritas.com.

Library of Congress Control Number: 2021907019

ISBN 9780578833712
EPUB ISBN 9780578833729
First edition, 2021
PCIP data upon request

For Jewel, Otto, Jim & John—my Father—I thank you all.
And for my Mother, Mary Kaye, who told me
I possessed the soul of a poet long before I knew it.

Contents

Prologue	7-13
Lesson 1 - Ownership	15-22
Lesson 2 - Positivity	23-30
Lesson 3 - Fear	31-40
Lesson 4 - Courage	41-50
Lesson 5 - Intuition	51-58
Lesson 6 - Choice	59-66
Lesson 7 - Inner Compass	67-74
Lesson 8 - Humility	75-82
Lesson 9 - Listening	83-88
Lesson 10 - Discernment	89-94
Lesson 11 - Mentorship	95-104
Lesson 12 - Succession	105-114
Epilogue	115-117
Acknowledgments	119-120
About the Cover Art	121
About the Author	123
Endnotes	125

Prologue

Round and round I spun
My world unraveled before me
Up at Dawn: New Web

When you are on the search for an executive leadership coach, you probably aren't thinking, "Yes, but can they also write a haiku?"

Several years ago when I wrote that poem, I had no idea it would serve as the foundation for this book, nor that poetry would have such a profound effect on my approach to coaching. But as William Shakespeare wrote:

"The past is prologue."

With each new word I write about the past, a past informed by my work as a performer and poet, the insight I gain into the subject of leadership, along with my desire to coach leaders, grows deeper.

I believe we are amidst the Dawn of a New Web, in a world more interconnected and yet somehow more divided than ever before. Conscious, compassionate leadership is critical. The world needs emotionally aware and spiritually awake leaders. Leaders are not, however, just CEOs. Leaders perform a myriad of roles. We come in all shapes and sizes; age and titles are of no consequence, nor is color, gender or sexual identity. If you think or feel you are a leader, chances are you are one.

Leadership, Distilled is designed to get you contemplating how you apply your wisdom and authority, while also encouraging you to take simple, creative steps toward more enlightened leadership.

Poetry, the power of metaphor, and performance have all provided me with great purpose and have served as the foundation for my awakening as a free-spirited and unconventional leader.

While I hold the titles of Founder, CEO, Artistic Director, and Executive Coach, I believe my real authority, my *true voice*, stems from my experiences as a creative artist.

There's a little-known process called ballooning—also sometimes called kiting. It's when spiders move through the air "releasing one or more gossamer threads to catch the wind." This propels them, making them airborne and places them "at the mercy of electric currents."[1] As a performing artist, freelancer, and sole proprietor of a business, sometimes that is how life feels—I entrust myself to the mercy of electric currents of creativity and let intuition guide me forward. It can be daunting at times, but the payoff has always been worth it. It has led me to bold new adventures every time.

> *"O, what a brave new world!"*

That quote, also taken from Shakespeare, captures the essence of how I felt (after ballooning from the East Coast to Chicago) walking into the corporate headquarters of one of the world's leading management consulting firms in 2005. As a professional actress with two MFAs, five years teaching at the University of Texas at Austin, and some rudimentary training in ESL (English as a Second Language) that I gained in the Peace Corps, I suddenly found myself cast in a new role as a communications expert and presentation coach. That day, I unwittingly stepped into a new kind of spotlight—directing and coaching consultants who also happened to be medical doctors, engineers, designers, data scientists, business managers, civil servants, entrepreneurs, and research scientists.

My background in voice, speech, and phonetics was brought to the forefront as I helped my clients craft and deliver dynamic messages. I would often tell them with a touch of irony that I was leading a "quiet revolution," aiming to create impact from behind the scenes. My intention was to guide each individual toward taking ownership of their true voice and beliefs. It was a stepping stone in founding my own coaching firm, Voce Veritas (which means *True Voice* in Latin).

From web to web, I shifted from being an actress, to being a director of my own firm, morphing into a fully embodied businesswoman. Embracing what I like to call *Artrepreneurship*. When the recession of 2008 hit, it hit hard. Everywhere. While it made coaching work scarce, it also provided me with an opportunity to ride yet another one of those wild electrical currents.

I granted myself permission to spin new webs. I took the opportunity to kite back to my home state of Minnesota with my husband. It was a powerful move. In time, however, as I continued coaching private clients, hustling between various industrious webs of performance and running businesses, I found myself in a place of imbalance. I was doing too many things. My world began unraveling before me. So I contemplated my ethos and made some serious changes. I sought solace and clarity in writing haiku. (Several of the poems in this book were written during that time.) All the while, I was gathering ever more information and experiences to take back into the corporate web. Little did I know—I was setting *my* true voice free.

I began writing in earnest, keeping in mind the mantra: *write what you know*. Of the plays and poems I worked on during those years, the most meaningful character I created was Miss Myrna Davenport—a substitute teacher who inspires students/audiences through her love of poetry and her unique style of bringing music and dance—the creative arts—into the classroom. Some of the world's greatest leaders are the unsung heroes of our classrooms guiding our youth. Myrna is my homage to them. As Miss Myrna, I said to my audiences each night, "poetry is life distilled to its barest essence." Little did I know the prologue I was crafting.

More new webs were taking shape. With each new endeavor, I created and led with more clarity and creativity. I returned to coaching renewed, refreshed, and with a new style: poetry in motion. I began using metaphor more deeply than ever in my coaching practice. I expanded the programs I taught, and I began traveling and coaching internationally. I was also learning the fine art of doing one thing, spinning just one web, at a time.

While I have worked with leaders in a variety of industries, I don't always get the time with them that I would like. As the pandemic that began in 2020 ensued, and travel was no longer an option, it dawned on me that now was the time to "kite" again and use this gift of time in my own web. Weaving the gossamer threads of my experience into this book.

Leadership, Distilled takes twelve recurring, dominant threads I have both experienced and borne witness to and distills them—filtering each lesson through the lens of original haiku and personal stories from the field.

Why the haiku? Because I believe there is great value in a succinct lesson. And there is almost nothing more distilled than the seventeen syllables of a haiku. If you are not familiar with them, they originated in Japan. Here again I see, the *past is prologue*. Growing up, my father did a great deal of business in Japan. His Japanese colleagues and their families spent weeks in our home in Minneapolis, visiting and creating a beautiful cultural exchange. In graduate school, I had the privilege of studying in Toga Mura, Japan and performing under the direction of Tadashi Suzuki. To say the culture has influenced my life is an understatement. In honor of that, I find myself deeply indebted to the brilliant artist, Chaco Terada, for permitting her work *Red Focus I* to serve as the cover art for this book. It, along with the simple form of the haiku, captures the very essence of precision and flow I seek for you to experience as you read.

I encourage you to take this book as it comes. Follow your intuition: kite through it as you wish. Read it in one sitting and return to the lessons when you feel called to do so, or spread it out over twelve weeks, or even twelve months. You could also move through it with a trusted cohort and create an ensemble of leaders who wish to put both leadership and poetry in motion simultaneously. I also highly recommend using the space following the practice sections to write about any electrical currents of creativity you experience. Put into words any discoveries you make about yourself as a leader.

However you approach it, may the one big impact be your feeling, as the Japanese would say, *hara hachi bu.* 80% full with 20% space to digest and grow: Nourished enough to set your true voice free.

Lesson 1

Ownership

I know a Zebra
who gave birth to herself and
became a Phoenix

Often, when I am coaching, I use metaphors to help people take ownership of who they are and what they bring into the room.

I wrote this haiku for a friend and colleague. I had the honor of serving as a mentor and guide of sorts as she was onboarding with a company where we both freelance. During one of our initial co-deliveries in Silicon Valley, she shared a childhood story where kids called her a zebra because of her mixed race. Suffice to say, this and other derogatory names she endured had an impact on her. As she bravely recalled her story for the group we were training, it dawned on me that while she may have at one time been called a zebra, it was clear she no longer, if ever, identified with that.

Her skin color (and other people's opinions on that) did not inhibit her, and her feelings about those things in the past did not set her back. Instead, she took ownership of who and what she is—an intelligent, determined, disciplined woman who gave birth to herself in an unstoppable new form: a phoenix.

Time and time again, I see great leaders give birth to themselves. It often happens after a symbolic fire of sorts—and from the ashes, leaders are reborn into something new.

In 2014, I departed from a company that I had dedicated a significant portion of my life to, and in some ways, it felt like my world was unraveling. If you read the prologue, you'll know the metaphor that made sense for me at the time was a spider. I had been whirling, which some spiders do when they sense danger. (It's a defense strategy.) Spiders are industrious, creative creatures. So when I stopped whirling and got back to constructive spinning, the new web that I began weaving led me to many new endeavors: solo shows, teaching at business schools, traveling abroad to coach. These were transient gigs and relatively short-lived, but each endeavor served as a distinct and well defined new web for me when I needed it.

As a leader, regardless of where you are in your career, how would you metaphorically identify yourself?

Like a good haiku, it may reflect the natural world—a zebra, a phoenix, a spider—fill in the blank. In my role as a leader, I see myself as a

_____

If metaphors are challenging for you, try these tactics: if you're into comics, movies, or literature, pick a character you identify with from one of your favorite stories. If sports are your jam, follow that lead. A good metaphor will be something that accurately reflects you. It will also light you up; you will feel the enthusiasm in your body and voice when you talk about it. So will others.

That's the first practice I want you to take on. See if you can find a metaphor that identifies where you are at right now. Sit quietly and see if anything pops into your mind. At one point in my life, I tried this exercise, and the craziest image floated up: an octopus. My sister—the wise woman that she is—said, "Oh, that's a no-brainer. You're starting to write your show." It was clear to her that I was entering a space where I would need to supply my own ink, like an octopus. I then researched the symbolism of the octopus. I was amazed by how much I identified with it. At the time, I was also longing to go inward. After years of a very extroverted lifestyle, I craved a quiet place to dive deep into subtle, dark realms that I hadn't ever experienced.

Follow your intuitive leads on this. See what parallels can be drawn, and then ask yourself, is it an empowering metaphor?

If it's not something that emboldens you—then choose something you want to become. Begin the journey of giving birth to yourself. Identify who you are now, and if it's not what you want to be, then give yourself a metaphor to morph into.

Remember: It's not a one and done deal. A good leader shapeshifts and takes ownership of themselves and their circumstances all throughout their lives.

Practice for Lesson 1

To help find your metaphor, fill in the following phrases:

I currently feel like_____.

I want to become like_____.

Once you have that clarified, start sharing it with colleagues, weaving it into casual conversations, refer to it when you tell people about what you do, and see if what lights you up doesn't light others up too.

Lesson 2

Positivity

The red-winged blackbird
despite snow and contrary
news returned singing

One of the first birds to return to Southeastern Minnesota after our long and often harsh winters are red-winged blackbirds. Seeing them instills a sense of joy and hope in my heart that can be tested by late April or May snowstorms.

In terms of symbolism, the red-winged blackbird is often a positive omen. They are astonishing songbirds (just as great leaders are often great speakers with tremendous range and versatility). They also demonstrate agility in their flight patterns (a nice parallel to leaders being flexible and adaptable).

Leaders are often in stressful situations. We sign on to lead regardless of the 'weather.' Any of your team could tell you: *your attitude is everything*. If you see people in your company needing an attitude adjustment—take a good look at your attitude first. What they are doing is a useful guidepost regarding how you are leading.

Attitude is more than just a mindset—it's about action as well. Are you physically and vocally demonstrating resilience? What language are you using? Are your messages aligned? If you are continuously stressed and anxious, it *will* ripple out to the rest of the company.

Does this imply you have to put on a false front? No. If a storm is coming, it's best to prepare everyone for it as honestly and authentically as you can. If that storm destroys things in its wake, you, as a leader, have the all-important task of setting the tone of positivity for the rest of the company going forward.

As I was reading a little further into red-winged blackbirds, I came across something that made me laugh out loud.

Environmental-science consultant Beth Kosson calls these birds "nature's assholes" because they dive and swoop at humans when they feel threatened.[2] This reminds me of a story of the ripple effect.

Not long before I began my work as an executive coach, I worked part-time at a hedge fund in downtown Chicago. It was a small firm, and they were quite open about their high attrition rate. While this should have been a red flag, I didn't let it deter me from taking the position.

A few months in, I began to get the picture. The fellow who owned the firm, a towering former college basketball player, asked me into his office one day, launching into what I believe was meant to be a tutorial. He began by saying, "Catherine, take a seat." Since I was fairly busy, rather than settling in, I rested up against the arm of the plush chair across from his mahogany desk and prepared myself to receive his instruction and then get on with the tasks I had before me. What came next was a bit of shock. The CEO leaned in and said, "Catherine, there are two kinds of people in the world: Losers and Assholes." For a brief moment, I was dumbfounded, thinking: Did he seriously just limit the human race to two categories? And such narrow, pessimistic ones at that? Without really thinking I retorted, "So what does that make you?" Needless to say, my tenure at the firm came to an end shortly after that. But get this: I wasn't fired. I quit. And the first, second, and third times I said I was resigning, the CEO (the very same person of Losers and Assholes fame) said, "You can't do that." It was so odd. Why would you want to retain an employee who was so deeply unhappy?

The moral here? There is actually more than one. First, there are far more than two kinds of people. If you are a leader holding a similar mindset of the world only being filled with losers and assholes, my advice to you is to hire an executive coach *pronto*. It's time to up your emotional intelligence.

Second, don't *be* an asshole. Take the counsel imbued by the better half of the red-winged blackbird. Accentuate the positive. After a long hard winter, red-winged blackbirds serve as a harbinger for other birds to follow. They also protect their nests.

For this lesson, take the critical step of observing your company members, listen to their language, see if their actions possess a sense of hope and joy. If your firm has a high attrition rate, look to your own behavior as the bellwether. If your company members are miserable, ask yourself "how am I contributing to that?" If it's an outside circumstance, like the pandemic, an economic downturn, or a particularly challenging time in terms of politics or the environment, ask yourself what you can do to remind them Spring is coming.

Practice for Lesson 2

First, observe your team and their attitudes. Take the time to write down a list of their descriptors (behaviors and attitudes you observe them manifesting.)

Second, implement a 360° review of your work—meeting one-on-one with various members of your organization, asking for their insight on your attitude. (If you need help with this step, this is the exact type of situation in which you can hire a coach like me.)

Third, test your agility and see if you can take a situation where you are feeling negatively and see it from another, more positive perspective. Once you have shifted your attitude, note how your behaviors change as well. Then, check back in with people who gave you feedback and see if they are experiencing the ripple effect.

Lesson 3

Fear

Deep Fear rises up
threatens like a tidal wave
Get ready to Swim

As a coach, I often ask people about their values. If I know what a person values (what metaphorical pool they swim in), I feel like I can connect with them and guide them toward their aspirations and ideals. Leading them beyond mere floating, and coaching them toward Olympic style maneuvers.

Not long ago, I caught the tail end of a fascinating radio interview with actor James Earl Jones. His words struck me because it was clear what waters he swims in. He said something to the effect, that in order to truly identify with, and know someone, he asks people what they fear.

This was a big aha moment for me: While values drive us forward, fear can be what holds us back.

As a coach, dealing with fear requires great sensitivity to your client's willingness to be vulnerable. In a group setting, that may take more finesse, empathy, and awareness from all parties.

Saying yes to coaching is like saying yes to swimming lessons: It's a survival technique. Fear can—and often does—drown us. In formal swimming lessons, there is that moment when the instructor lets you float on your own; it is paradoxically a very vulnerable and equally empowering moment *combined.*

My question for you is: What physically happens to you when you feel fear? We each have particular, visceral reactions to fear. Think fight or flight here—for most of us, our breathing pattern changes—radically. That's a classic indicator of the flight, fight, and, as I like to say, "deer in the headlights" response. The technical term is actually freeze, but the deer in the headlights is an image many of us know well. They look like statues—no breath whatsoever. We, too, react the same way. We stop breathing and a rigidity sets in—sometimes we literally don't move if fear is coursing through us—even if it's not a life-threatening situation. The next thing we know—wham! We get hit by something. And because we stiffened with fear—the outcome is usually worse than if we remained nimble.

Make a list of what you fear—large or small. (It's important to note here your fear may also be of presumably positive things, like success.) Keep in mind your body doesn't necessarily react logically—but it does react both physically and emotionally. As you are writing about things you fear (logical or not), notice what physically transpires in your body.

I had a rollover car accident a few years back. Harsh sleet, paired with 40 mile per hour winds, and black ice on a rural, county road with little to no windbreak set the scene for my car spinning out—and me preparing for the great beyond. It was terrifying. After three full rolls, the windshield shattering, I amazingly landed upright and mostly unscathed. Then...my mind and body began processing the incident. For some time after, just thinking about it caused a tightening in my chest and shallow breath. Occasionally, if the weather is inclement, and the driver of the car I am in hits the brakes quickly, the small of my back and solar plexus still seize up. My hands grip tightly. My body reacts much like it did when I realized my car was about to roll. Even in the comfort of my own home, watching a film or show and a car accident takes place on the screen, I still physically recoil.

I have taken the time to note these things because they can, each in their own way, inhibit me from moving forward beyond my fear. In fact, being aware of these physical reactions helped me deal with another radically different situation when I was coaching.

A few months after the accident, I was working with a group in an Executive Education program at a prominent business school. The person who had been appointed as the group leader said something that was openly hostile and belittling to me. (I'm happy to say this is actually the *only* time in my coaching career to be confronted like this.) In reaction to the comments made, I felt a familiar response, a form of fear kicked in. My chest tightened, my lower back seized. For the first moment my breath caught and I held it. It was akin to that feeling of the car just about to roll over.

Much like what I did during the car accident—once I realized I was tensing up—I took a deep breath, and exhaled. I honed in on what was ahead and paradoxically also opened up my peripheral vision. I took in the whole situation. In a sense, I prepared for impact. I looked the leader in the eyes, I faced my fear and addressed the behavior. After that I said, "Let's take a break." I needed air, space, and time to process the situation. The rollover was similar. Physically, once I discovered I was unscathed (in this case emotionally speaking) I released myself from what felt like "wreckage."

When the people who witnessed my car accident and pulled over to help me called out, "Are you OK?" I said, "No, but I will be." When they asked if I needed anything, I asked for a hug and thanked them profusely for acknowledging me by stopping and staying present with me.

Similarly, when one of the other participants of the coaching program came out of the room during the break and asked if I was OK, I said, "No, but I will be. Thanks for acknowledging how difficult that was for me."

Though my fear level for each situation was different, my body reacted in a comparable fashion. My instincts during the fear and after the release of each event were startlingly alike.

It was then that I could go back into the room, just as I got into a car the day after my wreck, and drove ahead safely—now imbued with greater awareness.

Life is full of things to fear, and we can't control them all. We can, however, notice our bodily reactions and our thought patterns. It is from there that we can learn new ways of coping. Which are akin to learning to swim.

If you know how to swim, can you recall those first moments when you were in the water, when someone let go of you? There's a freedom that comes when you realize you are no longer in danger. It floods through your whole body; you find a new strength. You begin to realize fear will not drown you, and it's at that moment that you are ready to rise up to meet the challenge of the waves.

Practice for Lesson 3

Take time to chart your physical reactions to extreme situations and emotions. Whether it's work-related or not. After doing so, seek parallels like the one I faced with the car accident and the challenge in the classroom.

See if you can craft a brief story drawing comparisons for others in your organization. Then share it with them.

Let these tasks be a starting point for awareness and alignment.

Lesson 4

Courage

Do you hear that roar?
Life's not for the faint of Heart
Courage is calling

I believe our greatest lessons in courage come from either having seen it in action, or putting it into action for ourselves.

When you think of the word courage, who comes to mind? Have you personally witnessed someone acting courageously? If so, what did they specifically do that demonstrated courage? When have you acted courageously? What specific actions did you take to embody it?

To be courageous is not to be without fear. It is to walk hand in hand with fear into whatever fire lies ahead.

Interestingly, the word courage comes from the Latin word *cor*, which means heart. And many extraordinary acts of bravery are often due to an adrenaline rush. The hormone adrenaline engages your heart and lungs making them work faster, which, in turn, sends more oxygen to your major muscles. As a result, you get a temporary boost of strength, and perhaps even a form of presence that is *only* demanded of us in the most extreme, and scary situations.

That is not to imply firefighters and others who rush into danger do not possess courage. They are trained to harness the combination of adrenaline *and* bravery. The pain or danger ahead does not deter them from taking action. They knowingly choose to walk hand in hand with fear to protect and serve others. Which makes their actions the very essence of courage: heightened awareness and selflessness combined; bravery that stems quite literally and figuratively from the heart!

As a starting place to examine some of your fears, consider that studies have revealed public speaking ranks higher as a fear than dying. Take a moment, and ask yourself: What scares me more, the thought of rushing out to save someone in danger—OR—talking with someone directly about an uncomfortable topic? Is the thought of being unacknowledged and unrecognized, sitting in the metaphorical dark, more frightening—OR—would speaking to a large group with a spotlight on my face be the greater fear?

If you feel inspired at this point, put the book down and jot down a few thoughts on these questions in a journal or in the blank pages provided, following each practice section. If you are up for it, name some things you fear. Then take the next step and write in more depth about those things that scare you. Take time to explore what your heart has to say on the matter of things you fear. (Take a tip from the previous chapter and note your physical reactions to this as well.)

Next, ask yourself if you feel vulnerability is a deficit. If you *do* feel that way, where could you practice small moments of safe exposure?

For many, it is on the homefront. Practice telling your spouse, partner, or a good friend how you honestly feel when an uncomfortable emotion comes up. Next, try it with a colleague.

I have worked with several culturally diverse, incredibly high achieving groups of leaders. Once when I was teaching at a highly esteemed Ivy League program, teaching storytelling for General Managers, I encountered a situation where it was difficult to discern if it was a cultural misunderstanding on my part, or an individual participant's fear of being vulnerable that stood in the way of what could have been a courageous act. (In all likelihood it was a combination of both things...)

During the 8 hour session, one of the participants told a story of a dream that they had about aliens. It was fascinating because the story had little to no impact without a critical (and comical) detail they refused to share. Since it was a small group who had been together a while, I gently asked them to consider telling us a little more. After a moment of consideration, they agreed to share it with us. It was a great moment when that extra detail was delivered—it was witty, revealing and deeply humanizing. Instantly, the group connected with them. The story came alive with the details that had been withheld up to that point. When I asked if they would keep that moment in for a larger group outside of the classroom, the answer was an unequivocal, "No. I would *never* allow myself to be that vulnerable with anyone I am leading. They would see me as weak."

The participant got so incensed by the suggestion of being vulnerable with those whom they led, they ended up leaving the room. Again, it may have been cultural, or the way I asked. Maybe it was merely the end of a long day—a lot of factors can lead to the decisions we make. But when they returned, it was clear something in them had shut down. Their heart was impenetrable despite the encouragement of their peers, and me, to remain open.

If I'd had more time with them, I would most certainly have asked more about their cultural background and explored ways of being vulnerable that didn't leave them feeling overexposed or as they stated—"weak." I believe balanced amounts of vulnerability serve as a model for emotional intelligence, and it is something far more leaders need to demonstrate. Ultimately though, each person has to decide where to draw the line in terms of emotional safety.

Another important point here is that using vulnerability as a strategy is *not* the same thing as being authentically open and honest. While it may be uncomfortable to be vulnerable with others, speaking truthfully and coming from a place of genuine connection strengthens your integrity as a leader. More often than not, your actions speak louder than words. Others see, hear, and feel when you are being honest. That, combined with maintaining a willingness to let your guard down—when the moment calls for it—establishes team trust and, in turn, creates a safe space for everyone to grow in.

Including yourself.

Because emotional intelligence isn't just about being empathetic to, and aware of *others's* feelings. It's also about being aware of and empathetic to *your own* feelings, and expressing your truth. Even if the truth is that you are uncertain, scared, or need acceptance. In revealing that side of yourself, chances are you will be perceived as human—which you in fact are—and isn't that the greatest truth of all?

Courage is knowing when to put the armor on and when to take it down and reveal your heart.

Can you hear the call?

Practice for Lesson 4

Think of something you feel is a weakness of yours.

Then imagine, or write out the following: If I shared this, then people would think:_____

_____

_____.

Note the assumptions you make. Reflect upon how this either holds you back or keeps you safe. If you have someone you can safely share it with—do so, and note if their reaction is what you assumed.

Write about the experience and see where you can expand being vulnerable.

Also, if you did some writing mid-lesson, review what you wrote and find someone to share it with.

Lesson 5

Intuition

A Conscious Yes
will open a place Within
where Silence Thunders

The word "yes" in and of itself is so powerful. The whole premise of theatrical improvisation is based on the term, "Yes and..." By saying yes, it means you accept something. You open yourself to the circumstances presented to you. The "and" is additionally a way of building. It may mean you build a counter-argument, and you do so without denying the other(s) you are interacting with at the time. It's a powerful form of inclusion.

Of course, there is a time and place for "no" or "but." As mentioned in the last lesson, boundaries and protective buttresses are important and necessary. Hence the word "conscious" is utilized before the word "yes" in this haiku.

How many times have you been asked to do something and automatically said yes out of habit or duty? How many times do you think those you supervise simply say yes to you because of those things? Have you ever considered that their saying yes may not be the full story? What would you uncover if you encouraged a culture of "yes and..."?

Recently, I have been working with one of the Big Four Accounting firms, helping develop a new training program for their newly appointed Managing Directors. One of the primary elements of the course is on building leadership presence. And it is often approached through the practice of role-play—which requires both courage and a conscious, open-hearted yes.

To make things a bit more realistic in one particular role play, I played the Firm Partner with whom they needed to push back.

In this instance, one of the newly appointed Directors had automatically said yes to leading a project that they knew was next to impossible to turn around. Essentially, they agreed to captain a sinking ship. Could they have realistically said "no" to it? Probably not, but their auto-pilot "yes," in retrospect, was something they could have done differently.

It was the perfect opportunity to role play and explore other options. Because they said yes without much forethought or hesitation, my first question as a coach was, "what values drove you to say yes in the first place?" After some thought, they stated that it was out of duty and loyalty.

Those are powerful reasons to say yes. Taking it a step further, and leaning into what James Earl Jones said, I asked what fear was behind it. They replied if the work were given to someone else, they would conceivably be overlooked for promotions. They would also not be viewed as a team player. Those are also potent driving factors.

So we replayed the scenario, each time we interacted, I suggested small shifts. The first adjustment was to breathe more deeply before speaking consciously and to listen to what their impulse was before speaking. Another tip was to act as if they and the Partner were peers—rather than authority and subordinate.

The conversation shifted beautifully. In the next round, instead of merely saying "yes" to the project, the Managing Director was saying things like, "This sounds like it's going to be a challenging project. Before I say yes, can you give me some insight as to how you would approach it?"

It was a game-changer. In this instance, saying no wasn't an option. But an unconscious yes landed them in hot water. They walked into a situation where the project was doomed to fail, and they had no backup. They instinctively knew it.

Intuition often thunders silently. We say things like, "I can't quite put my finger on it."—"I am not sure why, but I feel like it isn't going to work."—"My gut says...."

What about the times when you are asked to override your instinct? The thunder still rumbles. The storm *is* coming; your body knows it. If you have allowed an old habit of unconsciously agreeing to do a task, even if well-intended values drive it, chances are it will lead you into a storm that could have been circumvented.

Practice for Lesson 5

Think about how you learned to say yes, consciously. How did you do it? Did someone else empower you to do so, were you coached? Or, did you learn through hard knocks—the school of personal experience or self mentorship?

Here would be an ideal place to take a moment to also notice if you possess any biases about learning based on personal experience. Either way, how can you, as a leader, pass this conscious connection on to those whom you lead?

Once you have answered those questions for yourself, think back to Lesson 3 and note if you can associate physical reactions that come into play when you act with deliberation.

Now practice telling stories of times you consciously or unconsciously said yes. Manifest physical changes in your voice and body as you deliver them.

Lastly, so that you learn for yourself and demonstrate to others the impact of conscious and unconscious decisions—tell the story to someone on your team as a way to empower them.

Lesson 6

Choice

From Hibernation
into forced Isolation
Choose: Silence or Noise

Hibernation is a natural pattern. It's what many long for and go willingly toward—at varying points, we all need it. There are times I deeply crave it. It provides the downtime we need to restore ourselves.

When the COVID-19 pandemic struck in early 2020, forced isolation was upon us. For most, it did not feel natural. For many, it was unwelcome. (Although you have probably met or may even be one of the people who appreciated and even thrived within the opportunity that isolation provided.)

Either way, you must take stock of your proclivities: when something is forced upon you—how do you react? Do you prefer silence or noise? What do you do if your mind is full of noise, and you long for silence? (Or vice versa.) Lastly, can you actively find stillness amidst the noise?

Quieting the mind is no easy feat.

Try this simple Zen exercise to get in touch with how noisy your mind is:

>Find a quiet place, sit erect, inhale and exhale,
>>then begin counting to ten.
>Every time you think something between numbers,
>>go back to number one.
>Do this for 5 minutes and see how far you get.
>>Did you ever make it to 10?

Note what thoughts came up. What was the 'noise'—was there a running theme? Also, taking a tip from the last lesson—how did your body react to the 'forced isolation'?

A disciplined practice of quieting the mind expands your choices. Knowing how your body reacts can also give you great clues into how you both literally and figuratively move through the world.

A strong leader possesses clarity, conviction, and self-awareness—all of which stem from discipline.

Discipline leads to the conscious creation of new habits, to wise new choices, instead of old habits unconsciously dictating your life.

Practice for Lesson 6

For this lesson, I am going to give you two different exercises:

First, do the Zen counting exercise on the previous page every day for one week. Journal about the experience. Has your mind quieted? Have you noticed a change in your focus after this exercise? Note after one week if you want to continue. If you choose not to—notice what's getting in your way. Gain clarity around what works for you and what does not.

As a second practice, set a time aside for silence. Pick a day when you can set aside at least one hour and up to as many as three hours. Make sure this is a time where silence would be appropriate (in other words don't set it up on a day when you know a meeting may come up that requires you to speak). For those hours, turn off all distractions—your phone, your computer, music, TV, and let people like family and friends know you are doing this (lest they misinterpret or misconstrue your silence).

In the space provided, write about the metaphorical "thundering"—was the exercise hard for you? What did you notice? What emotions cropped up? Did you find yourself hearing, seeing, or experiencing things you normally miss out on? Note the myriad of ways in which silence is not quiet: Birdsong, cars passing, clocks ticking, the gentle rhythms of your own breath. Set aside another few hours and see where the practice takes you...

And remember: Meditation and mindfulness can be approached in very different ways, it's not a one-size-fits-all situation. Take time, and explore variation methods until you find one that fits your personal style. Then choose to practice it, moment by moment. It's not about perfection, or doing it right. It's about getting and being present.

Lesson 7

Inner Compass

*There is a Stillness
that drops in and guides the heart
It will find True North*

"Find Stillness!" Japanese Theatre Director Tadashi Suzuki is famous for saying these very words. A peer of mine said she once awoke from a sound sleep, sitting straight up, rigid and sweating, after hearing this command barked at her in a dream.

Suzuki directs and guides performers toward a harmonious blend of stillness and movement. He strives for moments of utter silence, juxtaposed with perfectly wrought delivery of text.

His work is profound and riveting to watch. He demands precision, and from that precision, blossoms flow.

Suzuki's command of stillness is not just a physical demand. It is about quieting a performer's mind and heart as well. The calm I discovered in working with him dropped into a place in my soul and opened my eyes to how I moved through the world.

I have been described at times as fiery and feisty, nimble and quick. In one business-based behavioral assessment, I was even deemed a "Maverick." Along the way, I have learned to balance these qualities with calm, cool, and a slower process. I strive to be both the horse and rider.

When I direct a show or run a workshop, I take stock of my nature and temper it so that each of the participants can receive the direction and guidance I am giving them. At the same time, I must remain faithful to my basic essence and to my principles—to My True North.

If you have ever held a literal compass, you know that the needle is continually adjusting. Yet North is always North.

When I was in the graduate program where I had the opportunity to go to Japan and work in person with Tadashi Suzuki, I spent many days and nights trying to get a sense of my True North. The program I was in had a very rigorous philosophy. There were elements of it that set my inner compass spinning.

One of the Professors once asked me—point blank—why I was there. If I didn't fully embrace the philosophy, why did I stay?

I was not particularly happy there. I could easily have left and moved on with my life. I had returned to school, not because I needed a degree. I already had a Masters in Fine Arts from the University of Texas. So the question posed was valid. What *was* I seeking?

I did not have the words at the time to express why I stayed. All I knew was that my compass was telling me I had farther to go before I reached True North.

It's an elusive concept.

It has to do with the alignment of body, mind, *and* spirit.

What I know from my own experience is, every morning and evening in my bed, before I got up or fell off to sleep, I would ask myself, as Hamlet did, "To be or not to be?" and every time I chose to be...*there.*

Not only was I learning by doing—I was learning by observing. While still honored (and apparent), my fiery nature was being recalibrated by stepping back, cooling off, breathing more deeply, and being still. With each passing lesson and experience I drew ever closer to my True North.

I always knew I was free to come or go. What a privilege! Ultimately, I stayed because I chose to do so. I was able to take time to discern my voice from theirs. Because I remained, I gained the all-important gift of awareness balanced with sensitivity to others' needs.

Tadashi Suzuki demands the discipline of his performers. They are trained with militaristic precision. It's an outstanding sight to behold. In the background, a pulsing Japanese Jazz plays, and the performers stomp in rhythm to the beat to the point of sheer exhaustion. There is then a deafening moment of silence and they all drop—dead weight. Slowly a *shakuhachi*, an eerie, haunting flute, is played. An elegant slow movement occurs among the performers, like ghosts rising from the ancient Noh theatre stage. In front of each performer, a quiet adversary and unseen challenger faces off with them. A private struggle that makes the performance genuinely compelling to watch.

They head willingly into the woods to find themselves and their True North.

One particular global consulting firm that I did a lot of one-on-one training for struck me as a working parallel to Suzuki's company of actors. They demand rigor and expect discipline. They also train young, high achieving consultants and actively expect a great majority of them to quit or move on after a few years. To be or not to be a consultant who gives 80-100 hours a week to their job, that is the question they face. The company's philosophy is not about work-life balance. It centers around the pursuit of excellence on behalf of their clients and, at times, the financial gain from that work.

Are you currently guiding your team toward the North of the company and the North of their souls? Is your company a training ground for some? What is your True North? Have you established a clear direction for your company? Is it well-balanced? Do you care? Are you allowing time and space for others to find their True North? Are they choosing to be there because they want to be or because they are afraid to leave? Take the time to ask. And remember: you, as a leader, serve as their guide.

Practice for Lesson 7

Imagine you are a guide. Where, and toward what, are you leading your company? This can be literal, metaphorical, or both.

If you were to script a TEDTalk, how would you describe this journey to that audience? Use images of cartography, the four directions and other elements of travel.

Lesson 8

Humility

Righteousness begins
a war that cannot be won
Can you Surrender?

As you have probably figured out by now, I possess a great love of words and their origins. The word humility is a gorgeous word that comes from two Latin words. The root of the word is *humus*, the word for earth—which implies a sense of groundedness. It also stems from *humilis*—which implies modesty. And modesty stems from modestia, "sense of honor," or "correctness of conduct."

It is a delicate balance between *humilis*—having humility and being humble, which is lowly—and being smug or excessively proud—those moments where you say things like: "*it's my way or the highway.*"

Can you surrender to humility? The very word *surrender* may be hard for some leaders to swallow. (It may be tied to the notion of vulnerability that was touched on in Lesson 4 on Courage.) For many, the word surrender implies loss. Here is where a paradigm shift and language itself can be beneficial. Consider this: ceasing to resist isn't necessarily a loss.

One of the world's most prominent consulting firms uses a potent mantra when entering a client meeting: *Be willing to release the agenda.* For the sake of what is happening in the room, for the sake of doing what is right, for the sake of all involved, not merely for yourself, and for the sake of building enduring client relationships—You must possess the willingness to surrender the agenda. (Yes—that very thing you have worked so tirelessly to create!)

It's a fantastic philosophy to teach people. Philosophies are only as good as the actions behind them. My question for you then becomes: Are you able to release your agenda, and ultimately your desire to be right, for the sake of what is truly good for all?

Saying "I am sorry," or "let's try it your way" and "I don't know" are not inherent signs of weakness. Instead, they are potent signs of humility and modesty.

Here's another image for you. At the Mayo Clinic in Rochester, there is a brass sculpture called *The Shamrock* created by the artist Harry Bertoia. Unofficially, it is called the 'Humming Tree' because it picks up the vibrations from the movement around it. When you place your hand upon it, (which you are encouraged to do) it connects you with all living things. It actually hums if you get close enough, but you must be very, very quiet and resist all distractions to experience it. It can be a very moving experience...if you allow yourself to be fully present to all the sensations stillness provides. Like this piece of art, a good leader is well-grounded, firmly rooted, attentive, and attuned to the vibrations of life around them. You also know yourself well enough to surrender your leaves and grow with each passing season. And, for good measure, keep in mind, the occasional pruning is a must for more dense, lush growth.

If you take a moment to be silent, observe, and maintain humility, what vibrations will you absorb around you? Reflect: Where and when might it behoove you, and those you lead, to surrender?

Practice for Lesson 8

Before going to bed tonight, picture a situation where you felt you were in the right, now repeat this phrase: *I surrender.*

Say it until you fall asleep. Visualize what the act of surrendering looks like. (e.g., apologizing, admitting you are wrong, stepping down from a position that you are not suited for…)

How does it feel in your body? Write about it the next morning. Did it reverberate somehow? How did the scene unfold once you let go?

Now, apply what you learned to a situation where you may need some humility.

Lesson 9

Listening

Listen to Listen
and nothing else: Just Listen
It may surprise you

As we just touched on with the lesson found in the sculpture of *The Shamrock*, listening isn't just an auditory experience. It's a full-bodied observation of something or someone. I would even venture so far as to say true listening is the source of intuition.

How often are your thoughts so pervasive that you miss what someone else has said? Be honest here.

On a scale of 1-10, how easily distracted are you? In this day and age, the day of multi- and switch-tasking, being fully present is difficult. What is it that you are paying heed to—if not the people or experience at hand? (Could it possibly be that you are listening for your next opportunity to speak?)

I cannot tell you how many times during the courses I have taught that people participating say in response to a listening exercise, "my spouse will love this." They are referring to the simple, but not necessarily easy, task of listening to, and reflecting on, what their partner is actually saying. The next time someone comes to you with a problem, before you step in to solve it or dismiss them to solve it on their own, consider this phrase: "Tell me more about that."

My sister's father-in-law, Jim, used to say this to everyone he encountered, and people loved him for it. He was revered for being an extraordinary listener.

Once you have invited them to elaborate, for the next moment, be sure to allow them one to two minutes of uninterrupted speaking as that is usually all it takes for someone to say what's on their mind.

If they get off track, guide them back to the issue with a question. Make no statements and no declarations of how to solve it. Just keep asking them questions based on what they say, not on what you are thinking.

It's a simple, powerful way to interact that may surprise both yourself and the person to whom you are listening. Chances are they will solve whatever was on their minds themselves and appreciate the space you gave them to do so.

Practice for Lesson 9

When listening to someone, especially if they have a problem, first begin with a new approach—ask them "do you want advice and problem solving, or do you just want a sounding board?" Regardless of their response, as they lay out the issue, simply say, "Tell me more about that."

Resist the temptation to interrupt them as they speak, and refrain from problem-solving or even commenting until after they have altogether had their say. If you must, take short notes of thoughts you have or things you want to share. Breathe. Hold off on saying them until the person speaking has had their full say.

Do this both at home and at work. After, write down what the payoffs were.

Also, note what things you didn't need to say, because the space for listening provided the speaker with the chance to discover that brilliant thought on their own—and because you created space for them to do so with your listening.

Lesson 10

Discernment

You must Distinguish
Wind from the Water—one Feeds—
the other Divides

Paradox! Which is it? Is this a trick haiku? Is it the wind that divides, or is it water?

You have read enough of these haiku now that the task for this lesson is to answer this yourself.

Practice for Lesson 10

Write on the topic of discernment and paradox.

How do you comprehend the obscure? Are you unsettled by contradiction?

Set a timer. Give yourself 2 minutes to do what is called "rush" writing.

Whatever this lesson provoked, whatever is on your mind, see where your mind takes your pen or where your pen takes your mind. See what comes up. Allow it to be messy and unstructured.

Ask a colleague to read the book, and when they get to this lesson, discuss this section in particular. See where you are aligned, and where you differ in your perceptions.

Lesson 11

Mentorship

When I first saw you
I never expected your
Blooming before me

I often have clients who are older than I am. One client, in particular, spent their career at the Mayo Clinic.

A force to be reckoned with, retirement for this individual is not about slowing down. They are tremendously thoughtful, well balanced, and tremendously creative. They sought me out as a coach for some speaking engagements on a highly personal and political topic.

I didn't have expectations around this process. I simply went into the coaching and applied many of the lessons I have written about here in this book.

The growth I bore witness to was exceptional. This individual blossomed in their writing and speaking.

It's not that I didn't expect great things. It's that I had no expectations at all. I simply responded "yes" when they asked me if we could work together. In a way, they allowed me to serve as a reverse mentor. This client has years of experience, and from the outside looking in, one might think they should have been *my* mentor, but being that they are a true leader—they approached me with humility and eagerness. (And, truth be told, they are a mentor of mine!)

When I coached them, the lessons I shared were readily absorbed and reiterated. I see many of my clients soaring after our work together. It's a tremendous feeling to know that I, in some small or perhaps large way in some cases, had an impact on their growth. And it's all because they opened themselves up and invited me to aid them in the process of setting their true voices free.

As a leader, have you ever looked at someone and thought, "no way," assuming you clearly see their lack of potential? Only to see them stepping up to the plate and knocking it out of the park?

Who is it you take under your wing? What are your biases and preferences? Are there times when you actively shy away from mentoring people? Does age play a factor in whom you choose to mentor? (And conversely would you allow yourself to be mentored by someone decades younger than you?)

I ask you to take some time to reflect upon these things.

Mentorship is critical for forward momentum—for creating space for great new leaders to rise up.

When I was young, I attended St. John's University Leadership Camp for Girls. I began attending when I was nine years old. The first year I went with a friend, and for several years after that, I went on my own. When I turned sixteen, I had my chance to become a counselor at the camp—making it the first job I ever held.

Father Otto, who ran the camp, was gregarious, athletic, open-hearted, and possessed a zealous spirit for life. He held a firm belief that athletics held a key to leadership: being physically fit, learning how to be a part of a team, how to compete and hold your own, how to win a game with dignity, and how to lose with grace all served as foundations to our training.

For seven straight intense days, we played racquetball, softball, basketball, and ran track. We swam and competed in the Olympic-sized pool on campus—where we learned to dive on the high dives and platform. We swam in Lake Sagatagan, hiked out to the Stella Maris chapel in the dense woods, and listened to old ghost stories (told by Father Otto) that scared the bejeezus out of us. A well-rounded camp, we also did arts and crafts and had a talent night. It was, on some levels, typical camp fare. But the level of competition in the sports could be fierce. There was a palpable desire to win among many of us.

I sought those blue ribbons, particularly in athletics, with fervor, and I thrived. I threw myself into each activity with wild abandon. Nothing was off-limits. There was no one there who discouraged any of my pursuits.

At the end of the week, Father Otto held a closing ceremony where ribbons were handed out. I have to laugh because I recently discovered I still have several of them.

Those ribbons, however, are nothing compared to the mentorship Otto provided me. In that ceremony, there was the final Camper of the Week Award. Father Otto prefaced its distribution by saying, "there are many of you who are deserving of this award." My heart soared. I wanted it so badly, but I worked to quiet my heart and listen as he went on...

"But today, there is only one ribbon being handed out."

Me. Me. Let it be me.

Then Otto said this: "Know this, there are far greater awards,"

Wait, what? What is he talking about...?

He continued, "The greatest award is the one God holds for you. There is also the one you hold for yourself. You, and you alone, know if you have achieved this award of leadership. True leaders don't need ribbons. They may seek them, but they do not need them."

At that moment, I knew another girl would receive the award. I also knew I did not need a ribbon to affirm a place of leadership for myself. At the age of nine, Father Otto gave me a gift that would last my entire life.

Not only did he serve as a mentor to me, but he also taught me how to mentor and have faith in myself.

Please note, this is not a plug for any specific religious belief here, but rather it is about the awakening of faith and belief in your abilities. If that faith is connected to an outside spiritual practice that can be very powerful. It is, however, my belief that faith—in and of itself—is the actual game-changer.

Take time to consider the following questions: What type of mentor are you? What lessons would you like to pass on to others? Are you breeding a sense of healthy competition among your team? Lastly, when you see mentees blossoming before your eyes, how do you acknowledge that? How do you express faith in them? And last but not least, are you actively demonstrating faith in your own abilities?

Practice for Lesson 11

Openly acknowledge someone's growth. First write about (or even to) the person what qualities they possess that you admire. What values do they hold that you see will serve them well going forward? Think about how they will receive this message best — is it in private? Will it be in writing, or would they benefit most by hearing the praise out loud in front of others? Deliver the message, and afterwards write about the experience.

Consider making praise a routine practice.

If you are having a crisis in confidence, consider doing this exercise with yourself as the subject.

Lastly, take a tip from the lessons on humility and vulnerability, and ask a colleague to do this for you.

Lesson 12

Succession

Truth is: come what may
the River of Life flows on
What will your wake be?

The word succession means "a following after."

I always laugh when I hear people say, "if I die..." and my next thought is, it isn't about *if, it's when*.

We are finite creatures. While I have hope for something beyond this life, succession is actually about this life, for those who follow us in it.

What do you want to happen here in this finite realm after you are gone?

Who will follow after you? What legacy do you want to leave behind? Who will carry on in your footsteps? Does this hold meaning for you?

I have observed great companies being run into the ground because leaders refused to give up their power and hand over the reign to others.

In graduate school, a teacher of mine once told my classmates and me that we were the "Death of the American Theatre." He wasn't kidding, and yet, a part of me smiled. While I know it pained him to watch us as we stumbled through his lessons—I took his directions seriously and revered his teachings (I had more than my fair share of blunders)—I also firmly believe he knew we, his students, were the future of the theatre. It was merely a future that he couldn't quite grasp. I sensed he was struggling with succession. Not only was his body and mind aging, but his career was also shifting. The world of theatre was radically changing too.

He came up in the classical theatre. Once upon a time, theatres had entire companies of actors, many stage actors aspired to be a part of them. You were an apprentice first, then you played the ingenue and young lovers, and then you stepped into leading roles. Perhaps you moved into directing when the time came, and then maybe even running the company.

The plays performed were written, for the most part, by dead white men.

Times have changed. That is the nature of all things. Things end and things change. This is the Brave New World.

In Shakespeare's final play, he deals with this very topic. In *The Tempest*, the lead character Prospero is an aging Magician who is face to face with powerful end of life choices. Prospero is a beautiful and challenging role. It calls for great maturity and a deep facility for language. I was cast as Prospero a few years ago. It was an honor to be offered such a part.

Speaking of "times have changed": It was an all-female cast of a traditionally all-male play—except for Miranda. (Miranda, in this case, was played by a man.) There was no political agenda per se with these choices; it merely allowed people to play roles not offered to them in the past. (A fabulous thing for all leaders to be considering in this day and age.)

In terms of succession, it's not the easiest story for me to share. It was the first time in my thirty-year theatrical career that I left the contract before completing the show. It was for health reasons. It was a very tough choice. I struggled deeply with feelings of frailty, humility, guilt, and even embarrassment. (I began identifying more strongly with my mentor from grad school.) Ultimately, I knew I had to take care of my body, and I resigned from the show, and my choice placed a great burden on the company. I was not without regrets around that.

Not long after I left, one of the younger cast members wrote to me and thanked me for doing so. She said in an email, *"I admire you all the more and am grateful for your example of taking care of your health in an industry/culture that often seems to demand that its artists sacrifice their mental and physical well-being."*

It was incredibly affirming. In terms of succession, it is precisely how I hope young actors follow in my footsteps—taking care of themselves rather than sacrificing their well-being!

In Prospero's final soliloquy to the audience, he says, "Our revels now have ended."

I cannot help but think that succession is about our revels ending. It calls for great courage to face that moment when the great metaphorical party is over—whether it's the end of an era, a company, your life, or simply moving from one role to the next—facing the unknown is, for most, unsettling and potentially quite frightening.

What will follow in your wake?

What traces do you want to leave behind?

I had the opportunity to visit that teacher of mine, Jewel, who told me I was the death of the American theatre. I asked him if I were to pass on just one of his many lessons, which would it be? He did not hesitate.

He said, "One thing at a time."

That is the essence of presence. As much as we may want to believe we can multitask, we really can only do one thing at a time. And that is where greatness lies—in being present.

That is a practice Jewel took to heart. He was trained as a Mime. He passed it on with passion and precision until his dying day. He taught it well. He taught with grace, humor and discipline. Because of him I now take great care to practice distilling what I do down to one thing at a time. In terms of succession, he did a brilliant job of passing on that lesson.

When you are no longer physically here or able to lead, how would you like your legacy to remain present? What final lesson do you want to pass on?

I encourage you to give that thought. To move consciously forward into the unknown, taking one thing at a time, savoring what is. That way, when it comes time to surrender and the revels do end, you can trust that those you have led will follow in your footsteps and forge brave new paths.

Your legacy *will* reverberate like the 'Humming Tree' and live on in the hearts and minds of those you led in ways yet untold.

The river of your life will continue to flow onwards. Perhaps in the most unexpected and glorious ways.

Practice for Lesson 12

Put poetry and leadership in motion.

To write a haiku, you use
>five syllables in the first line,
>seven syllables in the second,
>and five syllables in the third and final line.

First: Write a haiku of your own.

Second: Share it with someone in your company.

Third: Teach them how to write their own haiku.

That is succession!

Epilogue

In the prologue to this book, you may recall I quoted Shakespeare saying, "The past is prologue." That quote comes from—you guessed it—*The Tempest.* As you have read, the past being prologue has definitely been the case for me. Perhaps it has been the case for you as well. If you are a leader just beginning your journey—keep this in mind:

Our past informs not only the stage we are on now, but also the stages we will both build, and appear on, in the future.

When faced with the opportunity to play the role of Prospero, my body went into revolt. I believe in some ways I was not ready to play that part. If I draw the metaphor of *The Tempest* even further, it's clear to me the character I truly identify with is Ariel.

Ariel is the "sprite" who is in servitude to Prospero—they act as a changeling of transformation for everyone they encounter. There is magic inherent in the work Ariel does, and the characters Ariel encounters are somehow enhanced and enlightened through the encounter.

I work in service to others helping them shift their perspectives, to open their hearts, to somehow feel more alive, aware, and—yes—perhaps even transformed via an electrical current of creativity to a new level of being. Serendipitously, I contract with the Ariel Group based in Massachusetts. The work I do with them—teaching storytelling and coaching executives on their presence and presentation skills—is deeply informative to my private coaching practice. I am grateful to them for taking me on, back in the day!

While I continue my work with Ariel, I have also come to realize it is time for me to make my way steadily and mindfully into the role of Prospero.

My vocation is about striking a balance and owning my *voce veritas*—my true voice. And in doing so, I will help you find yours.

If you consider yourself a visionary on the verge of setting your true voice free—perhaps, you will be among my new clients?

As my epilogue, I leave you with this:

> *Our Revels are far*
> *from Ending, in fact, they are*
> *Just Now Beginning...*

Acknowledgements

This book, though years in the making, was born during the pandemic. Like many of my artistic works, the ideas steeped for a long time then poured forth. I am deeply grateful to the many mentors and teachers I have had throughout my lifetime and to the people who helped specifically make this work delicious: Stef O'Keefe, my editor and primary reader and beloved friend—you mentored me well, and served as a doula to this book, ushering it into the world with great care. You also kept my dashes to a minimum, which is no small feat. I cannot wait to bring your story to life next. To John Davis, you have been a champion of my work as an artist and a coach. I appreciate your constant support. Your feedback helped me craft digestible, do-able practices for each chapter. (Now...do your *homework!*) To my dear friend and fellow coach, Mark Dannenberg, you consistently inspire and delight me—your insights and edits are a gift, especially when it comes to Latin. To Megan Schneider, you will forever and always be my teacher of the year. Thank you for your thorough attention to my prologue. I know it's not exactly what you wanted, but I also know you support me no matter how I choose to express myself. To Christie Drescher Hepburn and Eric Hepburn, your feedback inspired me toward a new and what I hope truly is a stronger book. Julia Mines, you are a coach and storyteller extraordinaire; thank you for reading this book with such care, and guiding me through my fears. Judy Zimmer of Coachology, another amazing coach, and inspiring "Benny Sister"—your feedback helped clarify my mission. Johanna Rian, the day you asked me to teach with the Humanities in Medicine Program was a great gift to me—your insights and edits are deeply appreciated. Ian Jared Miller, you are a dear friend and true inspiration, thank you for taking the time to read and endorse my work. Sheri Brady, you were with me at the very beginning of my career as a coach...look how far we have both come, thank you for your support! To my brother, Futurist and Poet Jack Uldrich—your wisdom, gentle mentoring, and continuous belief in me has helped shape the leader I am. To my other siblings—Tom, your extraordinary poetry, especially your haiku have served as an inspiration to me for years. Thank you for demonstrating what it is to be vulnerable and loving on a daily basis. Nan, with your dancing, teaching and preaching you are a living breathing version of poetry in motion. Ben, your stillness and quiet watchfulness adds grace to our family; when you were adopted, you completed our family. For my brother-in-law, Scott Zosel, and sister-in-law, Cindy Divelbiss Uldrich, I couldn't have asked for better partners for Nan and Jack. You both helped shape the title! I appreciate your being supportive readers and audience members in all my endeavors. To my husband and the best listener and scene partner ever—Jeremy van Meter, thank you. Home is where the heart is, and you *always* have my heart, even when I travel afar. To my clients past, present and future—you enrich my life in both told and untold ways. Thank you for entrusting me with your stories, and adding to mine. Long may you bloom.

About the Cover Art

Chaco Terada is a Japanese artist based in Dallas since 1992.

The majority of her works use multiple layers of silk organza, sumi ink, mineral pigments and archival pigment printing.

The image for this book cover is a calligraphic painting over her photography, printed on paper. It is called Red Focus 1 © 2014, original size 16" x 11 ⅞".

When Chaco was four years old she began to practice Japanese calligraphy with her father, a master calligrapher.

She recognized the possibilities of her own artistic expression in calligraphy during travels to ten countries as a part of a cultural exchange program. By the end of her twenties she moved to the United States.

Since then she has been focusing on her inner life as a source for artistic expression.

Calligraphy became an energy to process and self-analyze her experiences, memories and feelings.

Her work can be seen at Valley House Gallery and Joel Cooner Gallery in Dallas and Photo-eye Gallery in SantaFe.

About the Author

Catherine Glynn is a leading executive coach and performing artist. She is the Founder and CEO of Voce Veritas—Executive Leadership and Communications Firm—and the Founder and Artistic Director of A.R.T. (Audacious Raw Theater). She holds a BA in Humanities from the College of St. Benedict and St. John's University, and MFAs in Acting from the University of Texas at Austin and The University of Delaware's Professional Theatre Training Program. She is a proud member of Actor's Equity Association (AEA) and the Screen Actors Guild/American Federation of Television and Radio Artists (SAG/AFTRA). She is also a certified Pilates Instructor. She has authored six plays and two books of poetry. Her coaching practice focuses on helping visionaries on the verge find their true voice. She works regularly with international consulting firms, C-Suite level executives, leading business schools, and Non-Profit Directors. Her clients include the Mayo Clinic, SGA Youth and Family Services of Chicago, Harvard Business School, and Yale School of Management, along with other top business schools and Fortune 500 companies.

If you are interested in having her speak to your organization or working with her privately, inquiries may be sent to: info@voceveritas.com.

VoceVeritas.com

Endnotes

1. Page 9, Wikipedia, "Spider, ballooning."
2. Page 24, Justin Breen, "'Nature's A-------', Red-Winged Blackbirds Known to Swoop Down on Humans", dnainfo.com, November 2, 2017

www.ingramcontent.com/pod-product-compliance
Lightning Source LLC
Chambersburg PA
CBHW031255290426
44109CB00012B/594